RAINFOREST
PEOPLE

Text and photography by Edward Parker

HODDER
Wayland

an imprint of Hodder Children's Books

© 2002 White-Thomson Publishing Ltd

Produced for Hodder Wayland by
White-Thomson Publishing Ltd
2/3 St. Andrew's Place
Lewes, East Sussex
BN7 1UP

Editor: Sarah Doughty
Design: Bernard Higton
Text consultant: Dr Paul Toyne

Published in Great Britain in 2002 by Hodder Wayland,
an imprint of Hodder Children's Books.
This edition published in 2002.

The right of Edward Parker to be identified as
the author and photographer has been asserted
by him in accordance with the Copyright, Designs
and Patents Act 1988.

Produced in association with WWF-UK.
WWF-UK registered charity number 1081247.
A company limited by guarantee number 4016725.
Panda device © 1986 WWF ® WWF registered
trademark owner.

British Library Cataloguing in Publication Data
Parker, Edward
   Rainforest people. – (Rainforests)
   I. Title
   304.2'09152

ISBN 0 7502 3869 0

Printed in Hong Kong by Wing King Tong

Hodder Children's Books
A division of Hodder Headline Ltd
338 Euston Road,
London NW1 3BH

CONTENTS

THE INHABITED RAINFOREST

Some people imagine that the world's rainforests are wild, uninhabited places. In fact, people have lived in rainforests for about a million years. Today, rainforests are home to over 150 million people, who live in settlements ranging from traditional villages to huge cities.

Many of these people are indigenous. This means they are descended from the people that first lived in the forest. Indigenous people usually live together in small, tribal groups and try to carry on their traditional way of life, which involves growing crops and hunting animals. But rainforests are home to a much broader variety of people than just the indigenous population. Many of the people who live in the rainforests today are migrants, who have come into the forest from poor areas in search of land on which to grow crops, or keep animals. Many come looking for jobs in industries such as mining, logging or cattle ranching. Most come from the overcrowded towns and cities that have grown up in the rainforests in the twentieth century.

◀ *This man's family have lived in the Amazon rainforest for more than one hundred years. His relatives first moved to the area to collect rubber from the trees.*

▼ *The Amazon rainforest is home to many indigenous people such as this Kayapo Indian boy.*

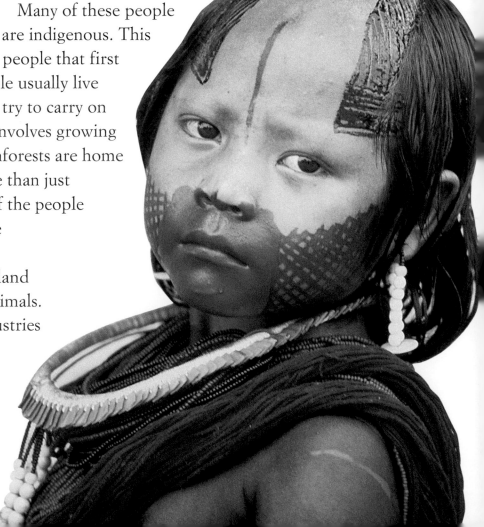

WHERE ARE THE TROPICAL RAINFORESTS?

The world's tropical rainforests are found within the tropics – a belt around the Equator, which lies between the tropics of Cancer and Capricorn. In the tropics, the temperatures are consistently high throughout the year and rainfall is greater than 2,000 mm.

The largest area of continuous rainforest on earth is found in the Amazon region of South America. This area of rainforest is similar in size to the USA, excluding Alaska. Rainforests are also found in Central America, Africa, South-east Asia and Australasia. This book will mainly look at the people who live in the Amazon rainforest.

◀ Local women walk along the edge of the Udzungwa Mountain forest, in Tanzania, East Africa. This forest is protected against deforestation.

▼ A map showing the extent of the world's tropical rainforests today, compared with their coverage 500 years ago, before large-scale deforestation began.

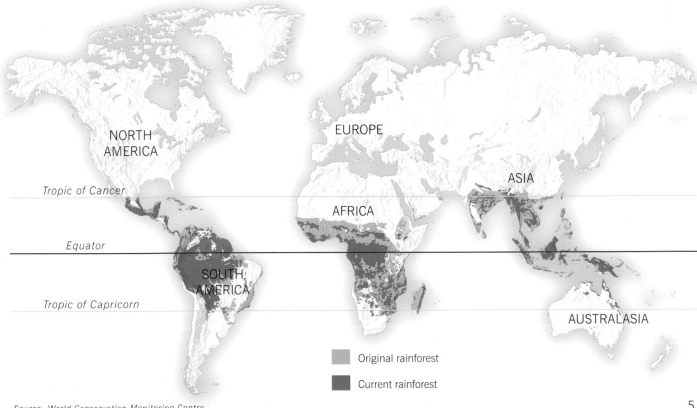

NORTH AMERICA

EUROPE

ASIA

Tropic of Cancer

AFRICA

Equator

SOUTH AMERICA

Tropic of Capricorn

AUSTRALASIA

■ Original rainforest

■ Current rainforest

Source: *World Conservation Monitoring Centre*

TYPES OF RAINFOREST

Scientists today recognize around forty different types of rainforest, but generally divide tropical rainforests into two main types according to their height above sea level. These are lowland forest and montane forest. Groups of people living there have developed different lifestyles, which suit the type of rainforest they inhabit.

LOWLAND FORESTS

Lowland forests are the most widespread rainforests in the world. They also contain the richest communities of trees and plants. Most indigenous peoples, such as the Kayapo and Yanomami Indians of the Amazon, and the Baka pygmies of Cameroon, live in lowland forests. These peoples have survived for thousands of years by carefully managing the rainforest resources. However, because these forests contain valuable trees they have attracted loggers who have cut down large areas of rainforest.

▲ A Woarani Indian in a dugout canoe in the rainforest of Ecuador in South America.

▼ An indigenous woman from tropical montane forest near Pasto, in Columbia, South America.

RAINFOREST SEC

THE YALI OF IRIAN JAYA

There are around 20,000 Yali inhabiting the central highlands of the island of Irian Jaya, in Indonesia. The Yali live on ridge tops surrounded by tropical montane forest, where they cultivate hardy vegetables such as taros, yams and sweet potatoes in small gardens. They also raise pigs and chickens.

The Yali are expert hunters and use poisoned-tipped arrows to kill their prey, including small marsupials, such as the tree kangaroo, and the cassowary bird, which is the size of a small ostrich. This Yali elder (see right) comes from the Seng valley in Irian Jaya. He is a successful hunter. The curved bones he wears around his head are the tusks of wild boar – a symbol of his bravery. The shells around his neck are for decoration and would also be used by the Yali as currency.

Fascinating Fact

The Baka pygmies of Cameroon can climb about 50 m up giant lowland rainforest trees to collect honey.

TROPICAL MONTANE RAINFORESTS

Tropical montane forests occur above 900 m on hills and mountains in tropical areas, where it is generally cooler and damper than in the lowland forests. The forests are often hidden in dense mists, which has given rise to their alternative name, 'cloud forests'.

Fewer indigenous groups live in tropical montane forests than in the lowland forests. Peoples such as the Awa in Colombia, and the Yali in Irian Jaya (Indonesia) have adapted to living in isolated forest. The lack of large navigable rivers, the cool climate and the unique varieties of plants and animals make these people's lifestyles very different from those who inhabit the lowland forest..

② THE DIVERSITY OF RAINFOREST PEOPLE

EARLY RAINFOREST PEOPLE

No one really knows where the first rainforest people came from, or how they colonized the forests. It is not easy to find the remains of the early peoples, because warmth and moisture in the forest have helped to break down organic matter, leaving few clues for archaeologists to study. Generations of people appear to have lived and died in the rainforests, leaving barely a mark on their surroundings.

Many scientists think that people moved from the savannah grasslands into the rainforests about one million years ago. However, in the Amazon region there is evidence that this area has only been colonized for about 15–20,000 years. But it is possible it may have been populated for much longer than this.

▲ Many Amazonian Indians, such as this Kayapo man, wear face paint and elaborate decorations for rituals and ceremonies.

◄ The remains of a complex of pyramids at Palenque in the rainforest of southern Mexico. It was built by the Mayas, at the peak of their civilization, over one thousand years ago.

THE FIRST AMAZONIANS

People of African origin may have been living in the Amazon region for thousands of years, leaving no evidence of their existence. It would have been possible for African fishermen to get blown across the Atlantic and survive the journey, or other great ocean travellers, such as the Polynesians from the Pacific, to have landed and settled in South America.

Most scientists, however, believe the first Amazonians migrated from Asia up to 20,000 years ago, and crossed the Bering Strait into North America, before moving south to populate South and Central America.

RAINFOREST SECRETS

SECRET SOCIETY

Some traditional rainforest beliefs have existed as long as the rainforest people, and have spread across continents.

Today, in the rainforest villages of Cameroon in West Africa, a cult known as Ekpe or the Leopard Cult is practised. It is a traditional rainforest cult, where figures dressed as leopard spirits (see right) perform energetic dances at ceremonies.

Variations of this cult were taken to other countries by the slaves who were forced to work on the sugar plantations of South and Central America and the Caribbean between the sixteenth and eighteenth centuries.

The culture of the people descended from African slaves lives on in the form of beliefs and cults such as voodoo, a famous secret society in the Caribbean, which is based on the culture of West Africa.

A rubber tapper in a remote part of the Amazonian rainforest feeding his pigs and poultry. His ancestors moved here from north-east Brazil at the end of the nineteenth century.

A rainforest family who are partly of Indian and partly of European descent.

THE START OF RAINFOREST AGRICULTURE

The first people who entered the rainforests from the savannah probably lived as hunter-gatherers. Rainforest agriculture is believed to have started in Africa about 2,500 years ago. A tribal group called the Bantu is thought to have increased in size around this time, and begun to move into the edges of the rainforest in search of land for agriculture.

In the Amazon rainforest, agriculture is thought to have developed around 2,000 years ago. However, it is possible that agriculture has been practised in the Amazon rainforest for much longer than this.

THE EUROPEANS ARRIVE

The lifestyle of rainforest people continued, undisturbed for thousands of years. However, colonists from Europe began to explore the world for new lands and trade in the fifteenth century. When they first arrived in South America in 1492, there were probably between 12 and 15 million Amazonian Indians living in the Amazon basin. Their numbers were to be devastated by centuries of colonization by European settlers who exploited the resources of the rainforest and its people.

▲ *A young Kaxinawa Indian boy in Brazil.*

RUBBER AND SLAVERY

The Amazonian Indians had already discovered the white sticky fluid from the rubber tree, called latex. The Europeans realized how useful latex could be in industry, and this created a 'rubber boom' in the Amazon. More than half a million people, mainly from the poor north-east of Brazil, headed for the Amazon rainforest in search of work as rubber latex collectors in the late 1800s. Many of these workers, plus tens of thousands of Amazonian Indians, became slaves of the Europeans. Large numbers died, either as a result of cruel treatment or disease. The lives of most of the Amazonian Indians who survived were changed forever. Many of the Europeans intermarried with the Indians, and a new kind of rainforest person – the *caboclo* – was created.

RAINFOREST SECRETS

CABOCLOS

Caboclos, descendants of indigenous people, and Europeans or Africans, are sometimes called the 'forgotten people' of the Brazilian Amazon. There are tens of thousands of *caboclos* living in the Amazon today. Many do not exist 'officially', because they do not have identity cards. Nor is their way of life as well known about as that of the traditional rainforest peoples. Many make a living in small fishing communities, while others collect rubber or Brazil nuts.

While many of the newer migrants who enter the rainforest convert forest into farmland, *caboclos* have lifestyles that are very similar to those of traditional rainforest people, causing little change or damage to the rainforest.

RAINFOREST SECRETS

THE MALAGASY PEOPLE

Archaeologists believe that the first people to arrive on the giant island of Madagascar, off the east coast of Africa, arrived about 1,500 years ago. They came from Indonesia and Malaysia in South-east Asia. Later migrations came from other parts of Asia and East Africa.

The island's inhabitants are called the Malagasy people and they are very diverse in terms of their origin and appearance. Today, there are 16 distinct ethnic groups on the island, nine of whom live in the rainforested areas.

The rainforested areas where the Malagasy people live are now rice paddies and look very similar to the land some of their ancestors left behind in South-east Asia.

CHANGING THE TRADITIONS

As European settlers colonized areas of rainforest, they also set up plantations and mines to exploit natural resources, such as timber and oil. They built places to live, roads and railways, and introduced new religions such as Christianity. These changes greatly altered the lives of the people who had always lived in the rainforest. In South and Central America, not only did Europeans arrive and intermarry with local Indians, they also brought millions of slaves from Africa to work on plantations. In Brazil, for example, an estimated 5 million slaves were imported between 1542 and 1850, and today many *caboclos* are of mixed descent.

Fascinating Fact

Within the first ten years of the twenty-first century, it is estimated that more than one million people will move from overcrowded parts of Indonesia to the island of Irian Jaya.

A family from the north-east of Brazil who have settled in the Atlantic rainforest which lies on the coast of the state of Bahia.

In the Amazonian city of Belem, a large part of the population, including this girl, are descended from local Indians and either African or European settlers.

TWENTIETH-CENTURY SETTLERS

Over the last 500 years, millions of settlers have moved into the world's rainforests, but the greatest changes to the way of life for rainforest people have occurred in the twentieth century. The main reason people move into the rainforests today is to try to escape poverty and overcrowding in towns and cities. Every year, millions of people migrate from the towns in search of land in the forests, which they clear in order to grow food. Governments of rainforest countries, such as Indonesia and Brazil, have set up programmes to encourage people to migrate out of overcrowded areas in this way.

However, there is not always enough land available for these migrants because of the way land is distributed. Migrants are not allowed to move to the best land, because this is already claimed by powerful landowners. In the state of Bahia in Brazil there are a quarter of a million people who are looking for land to move to. Many people have no other choice than to move to the Atlantic rainforest on Bahia's coast.

③ THE RAINFOREST HABITAT

THE VARIETY OF THE RAINFOREST

Rainforest people live in a variety of habitats, including the mangrove forests of tropical coastlines, lowland forest in the Amazon basin, and the cooler tropical montane forests found in countries such as Rwanda in Africa and Colombia and Peru in South America. Each is home to people who have adapted to living in their environment.

Traditional rainforest people have had to develop special skills to identify thousands of plants and animals in their habitat. They remember which plants cannot be eaten, when certain types of trees bear fruit, which insects and reptiles are poisonous, and how to hunt rainforest animals in the most successful ways.

▶ *A view of the interior of dry lowland forest, near the Amazon city of Manaus, in Brazil. It is often called* terra firme *forest.*

▲ *In the middle of the rainforest, most settlements are found along the banks of rivers.*

THE SOLOMON ISLANDERS

In many parts of the Solomon Islands, local people have a lifestyle known as 'subsistence affluence'. This is where the rainforest and the coastal waters are so plentiful in food that the people do not need to spend many hours a day cultivating, collecting or hunting food.

The diet of Solomon Islanders consists mainly of fish caught from the coral reefs off the mangrove forests, sweet potatoes cultivated in small rainforest gardens, and coconuts gathered from trees which line the beaches where villages are located.

DRY GROUND FOREST

Most Amazonian rainforest is *terra firme,* meaning 'dry ground forest', which forms part of a lowland forest. This forest has heavy rainfall, but rarely floods. *Terra firme* forest usually has soil that is poor in nutrients. Because of this, the rainforest people move regularly so that they will not exhaust the land. *Terra firme* forest tends to have only a few large wild animals per hectare. Rainforest peoples have learned to hunt the wild animals of the forest, such as deer. These animals hide well in undergrowth, and can move quickly. Hunting requires great skill and local knowledge in order to locate, kill and collect food successfully.

RAINFOREST SECRETS

LIVING IN THE FLOODED FOREST

People living in the flooded forest have cleverly adapted their lives to suit the seasons. For example, fish can be caught all year round. In the dry season, fish are trapped in lakes, while in the wet season, when the rivers flood, fish are caught from the rivers as they migrate to their breeding sites in the upper Amazon river.

Other activities also depend on the seasons. In the dry season, the inhabitants plant and harvest crops in their gardens and graze cattle on the exposed grasslands. In the wet season, cattle are kept on floating rafts while silt from the floodwater provides nutrients for the soils in the gardens. People can stay in their villages because their houses are built on stilts.

FLOODED FOREST

Some areas of the Amazon rainforest are underwater for several months each year. They are called the flooded forest or *várzea*. In the flooded forest, the water levels of the rivers and lakes rise and fall between the dry and wet seasons. In the wet season, the forest floods to form a large temporary lake in the upper Amazon.

Tens of thousands of people – made up of indigenous people, *caboclos* and settlers live the flooded forest of the Amazon. To survive, they have had to adapt their lives to this remarkable environment. They typically build their homes on the highest ridges of land. Their houses are built on stilts to lift them clear of the water in the flooded season.

Fascinating Fact

Some scientists believe that millions of years ago, the Amazon basin was a vast area of water, dotted with islands.

▲ *These men from a village in the flooded forest of the Amazon are making a dugout canoe so they can travel across the region.*

▶ *(Above right) A woman standing in her garden in front of an area of cloud forest near Pasto in Colombia.*

TROPICAL MONTANE FOREST

Tropical montane or cloud forests, such as those in Tanzania, Ecuador and Madagascar, are as rich in trees and plants as lowland forests, but the species are often very different. The undergrowth is much more tangled than in *terra firme* forests and this makes travelling around much more difficult. Unlike in the lowland forest, cloud forest people cannot move by boat on large, meandering rivers. The cooler temperatures also mean that potatoes and hardier plants are often grown instead of manioc (cassava), which is widely grown as a staple food in lowland forests. In general, life is harder for the inhabitants of montane forests and communities tend to be small and fairly isolated.

◀ A man climbs an acai palm tree to harvest the large bundles of fruit, which are sold to make a delicious drink rich in vitamins.

RAINFOREST ACTIVITIES

Rainforest people have many different ways of making a living. Some live in the remotest parts of the rainforest. Their activities include fishing, hunting, collecting wild foods, such as nuts and fruits, and cultivating small gardens cut out of the forest. Rainforest people spend much of their time tending these small forest gardens. A typical Amazonian garden will contain a large number of useful plants, including food plants such as manioc, maize, and beans, fruit and palm trees, and some medicinal plants.

After a few years, new planting is abandoned because the nutrients in the soil are used up. The people move on, leaving their gardens to return to forest. However, people will come back to their forest gardens for many years after they have left, to collect fruit from the trees they have previously planted.

▼ A typical rainforest garden where a small area of forest is given over to growing manioc.

KAYAPO INDIANS

The Kayapo Indians of the Brazilian Amazon have developed a highly planned system of forest management.

They have gardens near their villages where they grow manioc, tobacco, sweet potatoes and many other kinds of plant. As different crops mature they are harvested at different times, from several months to several years after planting. They continue to collect fruits from their gardens long after they have left the village to find more fertile soils.

The Kayapo Indians also gather hundreds of wild fruits, nuts and leaves from the forest, and many medicinal plants.

Fascinating Fact

Kayapo villagers from a large village may create up to 500 km of trails in order to collect forest plants.

OTHER ACTIVITIES

Rainforest people may also grow cash crops such as maize, coffee, cacao and cotton in their small gardens to sell to traders or as local produce. Some catch fish from the rivers to sell in local markets. These activities can be in harmony with the forest if the areas cultivated are not too large and the use of fertilizers and pesticides is kept to a minimum. Some small-scale farmers and collectors of fruits and nuts work for large international industries, for example in the rubber or rattan industries.

19

COLLECTING RAINFOREST PRODUCTS

Rainforest people collect a huge range of products from the forest. Most are food products or building materials. Foods such as wild fruits, honey, insects and mushrooms are collected to add variety to peoples' diets and to provide essential vitamins and minerals. Other useful products, such as vines and palm leaves, are collected to make twine, nets, baskets and sleeping mats.

Firewood and medicinal plants are also collected from the forest. Many of the products that are found in the forest are used by rainforest people themselves or sold to improve their incomes.

In the Amazon rainforest, international industries have grown up around the collection of a number of rainforest products. Tens of thousands of people are employed for part of the year collecting Brazil nuts and tapping latex from wild rubber trees. Other industries include collecting valuable palm fruits from the forest.

EXTRACTIVE RESERVES

In some parts of the Amazon, the government recognizes certain areas as 'extractive reserves'. People who live in these reserves use the forest in ways that mean it is protected in the long term, while also providing rainforest people with a living.

◀ A rubber tapper holds a ball of rubber he has collected and processed. The latex has been smoked to turn it from a liquid to a sticky consistency.

Fascinating Fact

Brazil nut trees do not produce nuts in plantations or in areas where the rainforest has been cut down around them.

▼ Latex being collected in the Amazon rainforest. The rubber tapper scores the bark of the rubber tree and collects the latex, a milky sap, in a small cup.

LINKS

Poison Medicine

Modern surgery uses products from the rainforests. One such product is curare, which is collected from rainforest vines that grow in Peru and Brazil. A colourless liquid called tubocurarine is extracted from the curare and used in modern surgery around the world. The way the chemical works is to relax all the muscles in the body with the exception of those that pump the heart. This allows surgeons to carry out delicate operations because the patient's body is completely immobilized.

Amazonian Indians have a different use for curare. They scrape the bark of particular vines, pounding it and extracting the toxic liquid for use as a poison on their darts when hunting.

Many of these reserves have been set up following the murder of the rubber tapper Chico Mendes in the Brazilian state of Acre, in 1988. Chico Mendes was a famous rainforest campaigner who lived near the town of Xapuri. This is where the extractive reserve named after him has been created. Within the reserve, people have the right to collect products that are renewable, such as rubber latex, palm fruit and Brazil nuts. The extractive reserve also has legal protection from loggers, ranchers and soya farmers who continue to destroy other parts of the forest.

◀ Local fishermen in the flooded forest of the upper Amazon catch certain types of fish using a bow and arrow.

▼ An Amazonian fisherman holding a tambaqui fish, which he caught using a harpoon.

RAINFOREST FISHING

Fishing is one of the main activities of rainforest people. The Amazon basin, for example, has more than 500,000 km of waterways, with thousands of small fishing communities dotted along them.

More than 4,000 species of fish live in the rivers of the Amazon rainforest, including the giant pirarucu and many different types of piranha. In order to catch the different varieties of fish, rainforest people use spears, bows and arrows, poisons and harpoons. Nets and fish traps made from local materials are also used.

Mangrove forests are particularly rich in fish species. They are used as breeding and nursery sites for many fish that are important for people's livelihoods. Small, traditional fishing communities are well aware of the value of the mangrove forests, and fish in a way that allows the forest to survive and the fish to breed successfully.

FRUIT-EATING FISH

Every year, the rivers near Manaus, in Brazil, rise. The Amazon and its tributaries together form a huge seasonal lake. When the forest is flooded, more than 2,000 types of fish swim through the underwater trees. A number of fish are adapted to eating the fruit and nuts that fall in the water. The people in the fishing community of Aracampinas, near Santarem, have decided to plant hundreds of fruit trees not for people, but for the fish.

A community spokeswoman for fishing communities around Santarem said, "Fish numbers have been declining because of deforestation and overfishing . . . Our community has decided to replant the wild fruit trees and to protect breeding lakes, so that there will be sufficient fish when our children grow up."

HUNTING

Rainforest hunters have to be very skilful. The number of large animals in any area of rainforest is usually very low, and many animals hide high up in the canopy. Traditional rainforest people have a number of methods of hunting, which include the use of bows and arrows, blowpipes, spears and traps. Most rainforest hunters make strict rules between themselves about when certain animals can be hunted, and to limit the number that can be caught. This helps keep the population of important animals at a sustainable level, and will allow hunters to continue with their lifestyle in the future.

Fascinating Fact

Fishermen in the flooded forest of the Amazon use a simple harpoon to catch giant pirarucu fish. These fish can be over 3 m in length and weigh 150 kg.

HOUSING

The homes of rainforest people vary from small, moveable hunting huts made from a framework of branches covered with leaves, to huge structures over 40 m long. These structures can house entire villages. The Mehinaku Indians in Brazil and the Dyaks in Borneo have traditionally lived in large communal houses. But many rainforest people, such as the Penan of Sarawak, are semi-nomadic and use natural materials to build simple shelters. These shelters break down naturally after they have been abandoned, and new shelters are built. In this way, the impact of the homes and villages of traditional people on the rainforest is kept to a minimum. However, the materials used to build rainforest homes can depend on what is locally available. In West Africa, rainforest people live in homes with clay walls, which form more permanent dwellings.

▲ A Yanomami village in Brazil. The main house in a Yanomami Indian village is called a Yano. It can house an entire village of more than one hundred people.

▼ The settlers that live in this house in a remote part of the Amazon rainforest have used local materials to build their home.

TRANSPORT

Rainforest people often travel over large distances. To do this, they walk along simple forest trails or travel by river. Various types of boat are built and used by rainforest people. In central areas of many lowland forests, people often use dugout canoes for transport. Along the coasts, many rainforest people have developed ocean-going sailing boats, such as the dhows used off the mangrove-lined coasts of East Africa. These traditional methods of transport are made from local forest materials and do not produce any pollution.

▲ The rivers are the highways of the lowland forests. Most families have boats to transport them around the forest.

RAINFOREST SECRETS

WAR CANOE OF THE MAORIS

One of the largest dugout canoes ever built is a Maori war canoe (or waka) called *Ngatokimstawhaoura*, named after one of the rainforest spirits. It can still be seen at Waitangi, New Zealand. Measuring over 30.5 m long, it is made from three separate trunks of rainforest Kauri trees. It is so large that it can hold 80 warriors.

In 1820 Major Richard Cruise, from onboard his ship, the HMS *Dromedary*, described the sight of a Maori war canoe in action. "The largest we saw was 84 ft [26 m] long . . . made from a single Kauri tree . . . propelled by 90 men . . . The canoe moved with astonishing rapidity, causing the water to foam on either side of it." The canoe is still an impressive sight when it is put in the water every year as part of Maori celebrations.

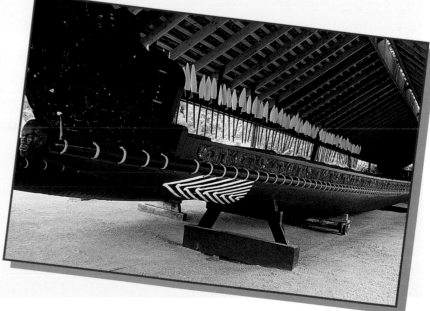

SUSTAINING THE RAINFOREST

There are many ways of using the rainforest in a sustainable way. For example, it is possible to use timber from a rainforest without destroying the whole forest. Unfortunately, loggers have already destroyed huge areas of forest. Today, some timber companies realize that if they do not use natural forests sustainably there will only be plantation forests in the future. There are also many people who are trying to buy timber only from areas of well-managed forest. These now exist all over the world. In southern Mexico, many community-run forests are producing commercial timber and chicle (for chewing-gum), in a sustainable way. In the Amazon, several logging companies have adopted a new system in which only a few valuable trees per hectare are removed, leaving the rest of the forest undisturbed.

▲ An area of forest in the Amazon, where commercial timber has been removed without destroying the rest of the forest.

▼ Each log from a well-managed forest is labelled and the number of trees cut from any area is strictly controlled.

RAINFOREST SECRETS

THE PEOPLE OF NOVEK

In the 1950s many subsistence farmers in Mexico were attracted to work in the timber industry, in the south of the country. They took jobs working for a big logging company, cutting down large numbers of trees and earning a small wage. In 1982 the villagers became the owners of the forest and started to manage it themselves as a community. Their area of rainforest, called Novek, has now gradually regenerated.

The people of Novek are receiving a much better income for carrying out the same type of work as they did for the logging company. They work in a way that cares for the environment, cutting down fewer trees each year than before. By cleverly managing the forest they can earn an income, while the forest is also being protected.

▼ These visitors are enjoying the rainforest scenery. Ecotourism in rainforests around the world creates local employment, and does not destroy the forest.

ECOTOURISM

Many tourists will pay to visit spectacular rainforests and their traditional peoples. An example of this can be found in Panama, where the Kuna Indians of the San Blas Islands allow tourists to visit parts of their land. The Kuna own the legal rights to their traditional lands, and can control the number of visitors.

For ecotourism to work, the interests of the local people and the environment need to be respected. Unfortunately, in Brazil the Amazonian Indians do not own any land themselves, and can be exploited by tour operators.

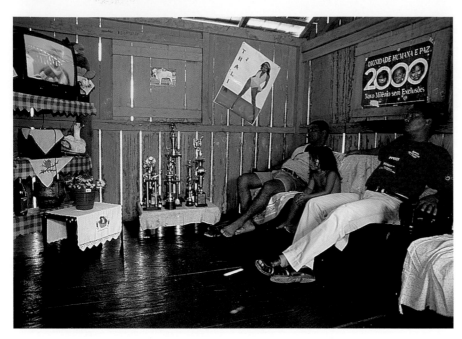

◀ *Some rainforest people today have access to satellite television. These influences are altering their view on the world, and in some areas, undermining their culture.*

ENDANGERED LIFESTYLES

The traditional lifestyles of many rainforest people have been changed by the activities of the powerful people who manage the forests. Today, many rainforests have roads running through them and they are plundered for resources such as minerals, timber and oil. Dams and pipelines are being built, and rivers are being polluted with toxic materials. All these activities make the livelihoods of traditional rainforest people very uncertain.

DISAPPEARING FORESTS AND PEOPLE

For people who live in the rainforests or who collect rainforest products for a living, destroying the forest means losing both their way of life and their means of survival. Where possible, rainforest people try to move deeper into the forest in order to keep their culture and lifestyle. However, most rainforest people have no choice but to become poorly paid workers for large landowners or to work in timber sawmills. Many end up living in the slums of rainforest cities.

▼ *Deforestation in the Amazon is forcing indigenous people to migrate out of the forest.*

▲ *Waorani Indians have had their culture affected by the arrival of missionaries in the rainforest of Ecuador, in South America.*

Another problem that threatens the survival of rainforest people is the introduction of diseases, against which they have no resistance. 'Western' diseases have devastated communities for centuries and even today, many rainforest peoples have no immunity against illnesses such as flu, tuberculosis and measles.

There are also other unwelcome influences. Rainforest people believe in respecting the forest, living in harmony with nature and using the plants and animals sparingly. Influences such as 'western style' education and beliefs often undermine the traditional culture and values of rainforest peoples.

RAINFOREST SECRETS

THE WEYEWA AND RITUAL SPEAKING

Lindi Mbartu is an elder of the Weyewa indigenous people, who live in a fragment of rainforest on the island of Sumba in Indonesia. The Weyewa have an ancient tradition of ritual speaking, passing on aspects of their culture to younger generations in the form of stories in their own language. Today, however, this oral history is threatened because young Weyewa people are taught in the national language of Indonesia. This is seen as a way of uniting a country that has more than 13,000 islands and hundreds of languages. But it means that part of the Weyewa culture and tradition is in danger of dying out.

RAINFOREST DESTRUCTION

Governments of rainforest countries often allow companies to cut timber and mine precious resources on a large scale. Sometimes they do this to help pay back money borrowed from the world's wealthiest countries. In some countries, such as Brazil, the government regards cutting down the Amazon rainforest as part of becoming a developed nation. People from outside the rainforest earn vast amounts of money by removing its timber and minerals. However, it is unusual for local people to benefit from these activities for more than a few years.

The main causes of rainforest destruction include converting the forest to agricultural land, ranching, logging, fires and mining. The building of roads, dams, pipelines and urban settlements also causes great damage. Rainforest people are often used as cheap labour or are presented as 'curiosities' for tourists.

▲ The timber industry is one of the main causes of deforestation in the rainforests, and has caused serious problems for rainforest people and their way of life.

SHIPIBO TOURIST VILLAGES

In Peru, tourists who visit the Amazonian town of Pucallpa are offered a chance to see 'real' Amazonian Indians. Tours are arranged to Shipibo Indian villages to see people making beautiful clay pots, decorated in the distinct geometrical designs of the Shipibo.

However, the Shipibo have lost most of their rainforest lands to loggers, colonists and ranchers, and their culture has been changed by outsiders. They now have little choice but to let themselves be offered as tourist attractions. Many people think that the Amazonian Indians should have the right to own the land they inhabit and to live on it as they wish, without having to provide a spectacle for tourists.

▼ New settlers move into the rainforest in order to grow food, and cut down large areas of forest. The land they cultivate is often not suitable for their crops.

LOGGING

Logging is one of the most obvious causes of rainforest destruction. In countries such as the Philippines, Thailand, Venezuela, Australia and Cameroon, huge areas of forest have been destroyed by loggers. Unfortunately, logging techniques are often very crude, which means whole areas are felled just to extract a few trees that can be sold. Rainforest timber is in great demand from Europe, North America, Japan and increasingly, from China. The timber is used as raw material in products such as paper, cellulose and plywood. This demand has led to massive destruction of the tropical rainforests.

The large populations living in some areas of African and Asian rainforest is leading to the conversion of large areas of rainforest to agriculture.

▼ Many homeless people, such as this man in the state of Bahia, Brazil, cut down forest to grow food for their starving families.

FROM RAINFOREST TO AGRICULTURAL LAND

Throughout the world, large areas of rainforest are being changed into agricultural land. However, soils are generally too poor to support crops for more than a few years. In some parts of the world, individuals may each be cutting down around half a hectare of rainforest every year to support crops or make forest gardens.

In West Africa, the increasing numbers of people who live in, or have recently moved into the rainforest, are causing serious deforestation. This is threatening the lifestyles of the people in the long-established villages. As there is only a limited supply of forest and an increasing number of inhabitants, there is a risk that the forest will be completely replaced by agricultural land. The new arrivals do not often have the same expertise as the traditional people in managing natural resources for the future. Areas of African rainforest, as elsewhere, are often cleared to make way for large plantations of commercial crops such as pineapples and bananas.

LINKS

Oil Palm Plantations

Many rainforest people have had their forests cut down to make way for oil palm plantations. The African oil palm thrives in places where rainfall is high. Commercial plantations (see right) have been set up in countries such as Cameroon, Ecuador, Malaysia and Indonesia. Oil comes from both the flesh and the kernel of the oil palm (see far right). It is now one of the main sources of vegetable oil and can also used in goods such as biscuits, soap, margarine and shampoo.

The African oil palm is well suited to rainforest conditions, because it can survive on poor soils. However, the soil needs to be treated with fertilizers to maintain its productivity. In many areas, it is cheaper

to cut down a new area of forest and create a new plantation than it is to pay for the fertilizer.

This has been a major cause of deforestation in Malaysia and Indonesia in recent years.

POWERFUL LANDOWNERS AND LANDLESS PEOPLE

In the Amazon rainforest, powerful landowners are rapidly clearing the forest for new soya bean farms. They are also forcing many Brazilian families to move away from good agricultural land, so that they can make their soya bean estates bigger.

In Brazil, 4.5 per cent of the landowners own 81 per cent of all farmland. However, most rural families own no land at all. Landless people are forced to move into the rainforest and cut down areas of forest in an effort to feed their families.

◄ A ranch hand rounds up the cattle on an area that was once Amazonian rainforest.

COWBOYS AND CATTLE

Ranching is one of the greatest threats to the rainforest and its people in Central and South America. Cattle need huge areas of land to graze in and they consume large amounts of grain and soya from huge plantations. Tens of thousands of hectares of forest in Central America have been burnt down to make way for cattle ranches. Much of the beef from countries such as Costa Rica and Panama is exported for use in fast-food hamburgers and in pet foods.

In the Amazon, ranching is a disaster for the rainforest and its people. This is because the forest is destroyed, ruining the homes and livelihoods of rainforest people. Furthermore, the number of people who are employed per hectare on the ranches is only a fraction of the number that could be supported by collecting nuts, fruits and rubber in a standing rainforest.

Fascinating Fact

There are 100,000 cattle ranches in Amazonia. Each animal requires at least five hectares of land for its survival.

34

LINKS

Chocolate and the Forest

Chocolate is made from the seeds that grow in the pods of the cacao tree (see below right). The cultivation of cacao has helped to preserve the rainforest and provide employment for tens of thousands of people in the tropics. This is because the cacao plants need to grow in the shade of rainforest trees. However, in 1997 cacao plants growing in the Atlantic rainforest in Brazil, became infected with a virus that quickly destroyed them. Thousands of people lost their jobs and much of the forest was destroyed to make way for ranching or crops, such as bananas (see above right) that do not need the shade of rainforest trees.

FISH AND WILD ANIMALS

Wild resources are often over-exploited. For example, large fishing fleets in the Amazon catch tens of thousands of tonnes of fish each year with little thought for managing fish stocks for the future. In African cities, the trade in 'bush meat', such as deer, monkeys and even manatees (aquatic animals) from the rainforests, is reducing food for traditional hunters and causing damage to the environment. The poaching of rare animals, such as tigers for their skins, and bears for their organs, is another threat to the rainforests and rainforest people.

▼ *A fish market near Santarem, Brazil. When the Amazon floods, the fish feed on fruit and forest litter. If the forest is cleared, the fish do not get the food that they need to survive and fish stocks will suffer.*

The discovery of oil in the rainforest of Ecuador has led to the pollution of rivers and the growth of towns like Lago Agrio.

BIG PLANS

Many politicians and large businesses often look at the rainforest only in terms of the money they can gain from it. They think an untapped rainforest is a waste of resources. International businesses and organizations often think in the same way, and have loaned large amounts of money to some countries to build roads, dams for hydroelectric power schemes, pipelines and mines, in order to develop the economy.

Many of these gigantic schemes have been badly planned. For example, when the Tucurui dam in Brazil was built, the developers did not think about the trees in the valley that would be flooded. Nearly 2.5 million cubic metres of prime timber was left underwater. The tannin from the trees made the lake highly acidic which, in turn, corroded the generating turbines of the Tucurui dam.

▼ Mining for gold. Large-scale mining in the rainforest is causing hardship to many local Indians and other rainforest people.

LINKS

The Road to Extinction

Road-building has had a particularly serious effect on Amazonian Indians. A new road between the cities of Manaus and Caracarai, for example, was built straight through the territory of the Wairmiri Atroari Indians. In just a few years, their numbers were reduced from over 3,000 to less than 350 people.

In 2001, the Brazilian government announced a huge road-building programme for the Amazon region, as part of 'Advance Brazil'. This will cause great problems to many other Amazonian Indians, such as the Yanomami and Kaxinawa.

Fascinating Fact

During the wet season, many of Brazil's roads become flooded and have to be closed to traffic. Some roads are even washed away.

MAKING THE PROBLEM WORSE

Road-building almost always encourages settlers to move into new parts of the rainforest. It also makes the situation worse because it speeds up the loss of the forest, and encourages increased burning along the edges of roads to control plant growth. More settlers help pollute the rivers and spread fatal diseases to rainforest people. It also means that the lifestyles of traditional peoples are disturbed or destroyed. In the case of the Yanomami Indians in Brazil, new roads allowed thousands of gold miners to move on to their land, destroying the forest, polluting the rivers with mercury and even killing Yanomami people themselves. Many of their groups now have so few people that the Yanomami may disappear completely from large parts of the Brazilian Amazon region that was once their home.

⑥ CONSERVATION OF THE RAINFOREST

The community of Aracampinas, near Santarem in Brazil, has built an environmental centre to teach children about the plants and animals that live in the rainforest.

THE SITUATION TODAY

At the beginning of the twenty-first century, the situation for many traditional and other rainforest people is very serious. However, many local people are taking action to try to improve their lives, while keeping hold of their own culture. Where rainforest people have gained legal rights to their land, they can choose how they want to live. They may combine their traditional lives with some of the advantages of the modern world, if they wish. This can include having their own medical centres, which offer western medicines – to deal with illnesses such as measles or flu – alongside their own traditional remedies.

In addition to local activities, there are many individuals and international organizations that are campaigning on behalf of rainforest people. They are putting pressure on governments, large companies and powerful landowners to recognize rainforest peoples' basic human and land rights.

In the town of Xapuri, local people have organized a Brazil nut processing factory, run as a cooperative, so that the whole community can enjoy the economic benefits.

COOPERATIVE ACTION

A number of rainforest people have formed cooperatives to sell rainforest products. For example, the Kayapo Indians collect Brazil nuts to sell to Fair Trade organizations. Rubber tappers in Brazil have also formed cooperatives and work together to help conserve their way of life. Cooperatives can allow groups of rainforest people to keep some aspects of their way of life and earn money to help the community as a whole. Some groups, such as the Kaxinawa, live deep in the Brazilian forest, but sell their goods made from wild rubber via the Internet.

RAINFOREST SECRETS

WOMEN'S GROUPS ON MAFIA ISLAND

The mangrove island of Mafia lies off the coast of Tanzania in the Indian Ocean. Here some villages have formed women's groups who have teamed up to make mats and baskets, to try to earn extra money by selling items to tourists visiting the island. They also fish for octopus to help pay for materials they need. They have built a storehouse and meeting room with the money they have collected. This is also helping to pay for a better medical centre or clinic.

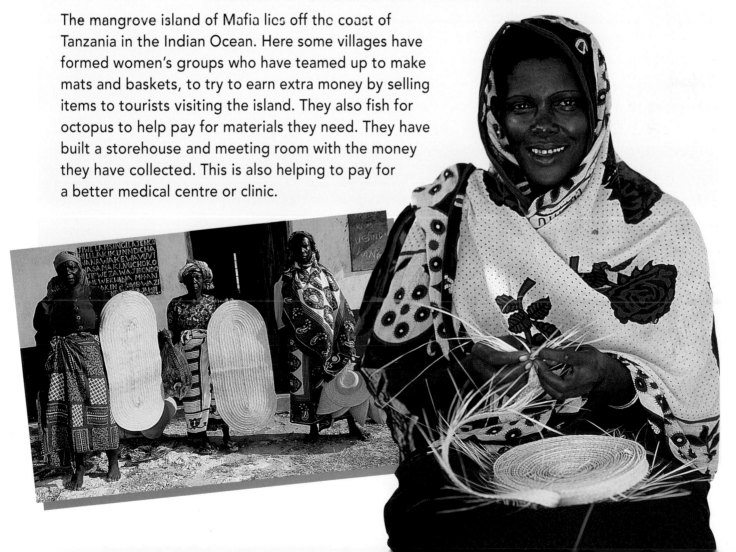

LAND RIGHTS

Of all the actions that need to be taken, the most important is to recognize the rights of rainforest people to their traditional lands. This is what rainforest people continually ask for. It is only by knowing they cannot be forced off their lands that they can have a chance of fighting against the pressures of the outside world. In this way, they can choose how they use their own rainforest resources and what aspects of the outside world, if any, they would like to adopt.

EDUCATION

The role of education for rainforest people is very important. In many countries, the kind of education that rainforest children receive is not well suited to their lifestyle. This is because it can undermine rainforest life by suggesting that traditional activities are not really valuable.

▲ A village near Andapa in Madagascar, where the community has gained the land rights and is now managing its own rainforest.

◀ WWF has provided environmental education training for many schoolteachers who work with rainforest communities, such as this one at Seringal in northern Brazil.

A FISHING VILLAGE IN MEXICO

In the small primary school of Celestun, a fishing village set in the mangrove coast of south-east Mexico, the children learn about the environment. The village revolves around fishing for octopus, crabs and a variety of commercial fish. It is important for the children to learn about how to manage the fish stocks and protect the mangrove forest, because fishing and tourism will be their future if they stay in the village. Some students will work in the fish-packing plant but many others will combine fishing with working as guides for the tourists who come to see the town's spectacular lagoon.

Some people suggest that it is not modern and efficient to collect rainforest products in a traditional way. Such views have led many rainforest people to leave their traditional lands, mistakenly believing that life in a town or city may be better. However, in other areas education programmes recognize that children should be able to feel proud of their own culture and way of life. They are also taught about both the benefits and the problems associated with a 'western' style of living.

In this way, rainforest people have the chance to choose their lifestyle and either decide to live in a traditional way or make a change. Organizations such as the WWF and Oxfam help fund rainforest environmental education programmes in remote areas.

The Chico Mendes Extractive Reserve near Xapuri in Brazil is famous internationally. It is protected from being developed, but allows renewable resources to be collected. It provides a model for other rainforest communities to follow.

CAMPAIGNING ORGANIZATIONS

There are many organizations that try to help rainforest people to survive and keep their traditional way of life. Survival International, Oxfam and Christian Aid are just some of the groups campaigning on behalf of rainforest people. They aim to protect their homes and help them gain recognition of their land rights.

Many organizations, including major religious, human rights and environmental groups, are calling for debt repayments to be cancelled for the poorest countries of the world. This would help slow down the destruction of the rainforest, which occurs when countries try to pay back large debts by selling their forest resources. The WWF has also successfully campaigned for governments of many rainforest countries to provide 'gifts of land' to traditional rainforest people.

Fascinating Fact

A letter-writing campaign organized by Survival International resulted in the government of Colombia granting the Nukac people a large area of rainforest.

International environmental organizations are supporting communities involved in sustainable use of their forests, such as collecting Brazil nuts.

INHERITOR CHILDREN FROM COLOMBIA

High in the cloud forests of southern Colombia, a group of children are making an impact on local society. Around a lake called La Cocha about 100 children have organized themselves into a group called The Inheritors of the Planet. Supported by the WWF, they have campaigned to protect their cloud forest from the practice of making charcoal, which is destructive to the forest. They also spend their time working on environmental projects, such as replanting trees. They meet and talk to other children about how to protect their rainforest, and in this way guard their long-term future.

WHAT CAN YOU DO?

You can help rainforest people by supporting some of the organizations which campaign on their behalf. Buying products such as Fair Trade coffee and 'certified' timber products is another way in which you can help their survival. These schemes that produce these goods all recognize the land and community rights of rainforest people and are working to help them achieve this.

⑦ THE FUTURE

UNCERTAIN FUTURE

Rainforests are important to everyone in the world, whether they live in them or not. The World Conservation Monitoring Centre estimates that 400,000 hectares of rainforest in the Amazon is being cut down every year. This makes the future of many rainforest people very uncertain. Although they face many problems, rainforest people are trying to find ways to solve them. In many rainforests they have been forming organizations to try to make sure that their rights to their land and way of life are recognized, so that they can plan a future for themselves. As part of this process, rainforest people have been putting forward important ideas about how the forest can be safeguarded, and how some of the damage that has been done to their forest and their traditions can be repaired.

◀ One of the young people belonging to the group called The Inheritors of the Planet, in Colombia.

▼ Collecting vines used for brushes and baskets. The future of rainforests such as the Amazon depends on everybody using their resources sustainably.

RAINFOREST SECRETS

THE UDZUNGWA MOUNTAIN NATIONAL PARK IN TANZANIA

Along the edge of the Udzungwa Mountain National Park, children are learning how to protect their environment and way of life. The park authorities let the children enter the park to carry out many traditional activities such as collecting mushrooms and fruit.

Two days a week people are allowed to collect fallen branches and dead wood for firewood. Children at the school are planting trees along the edge of the park near their villages so that they will have access to firewood and timber when they grow up.

AMAZON INITIATIVES

In the Amazon, rainforest Indians and other rainforest people, such as rubber tappers, have been working together to try to protect the forest and their lifestyles. In Brazil, a number of campaigning organizations such as the 'Forest People's Alliance' have been formed. This organization is calling for rainforest people to take part in government decisions. It also believes that people who colonize the rainforests should be taught how to live in the forest without destroying it. The organization recommends that large projects such as dams should be cancelled, and that the remaining forest should be protected for the future.

GLOSSARY

A cultural event by the Weyera in Indonesia.

archaeologists People who study human history by looking for remains of ancient human activity.

bush meat A term for meat from wild animals, which are killed for human consumption.

caboclo A Brazilian word for the descendants of a marriage between an Amazonian Indian and a settler.

campaigner A person who tries to raise public and political awareness about a cause or an issue.

canopy The layer of trees between the forest floor and the tallest towering treetops.

cash crops Products such as cotton and sugar, which are sold as a way of earning an income.

certified Wood that comes from an area of forest that is officially recognized as being well managed.

chicle The sticky sap from a rainforest tree, which is the raw material used to make chewing-gum.

colonize To move into an area and set up a new community.

commercial crops Crops such as coffee and soya, which have a high value when sold on the market.

cooperative A business owned and run by a group of people, who share the profits between them.

ecotourism When tourists visit natural environments with an interest in conserving them.

extinct When the species of any living organism, such as an animal, a tree or a plant no longer exists.

fertilizers Substances added to the soil to make it more fertile for growing crops.

indigenous Belonging originally or naturally to a particular place.

mangrove A swamp forest found on tropical and sub-tropical tidal mud flats.

nomadic A lifestyle of roaming from place to place, often looking for new pastures or agricultural land.

nursery sites Areas where young animals or fish grow up in relative security.

nutrients Any substances that provide essential nourishment for living organisms.

organic A crop or method of animal production that does not involve the use of artificial chemicals.

plantations Farms or estates where crops are cultivated.

poachers People who illegally hunt or collect animals, fish or plants.

rainforest garden A small garden that is cultivated in a rainforest area.

ranching Farming that is primarily involved in cattle-breeding and rearing for meat.

rattan The tough, flexible stem of a climbing palm, collected mainly for making furniture.

savannah Open grassland in tropical or subtropical areas where few trees or bushes grow.

slaves People who are the legal property of others, and are forced to work for no money.

slums Poor urban areas of housing, where people often live without good access to basic services.

species A group of animals or plants that closely resemble one another.

sustainable A way of using resources that does not threaten their long-term availability or the survival of the plants, animals or people who depend on them.

voodoo A type of religious witchcraft practised by the descendents of slaves in the Caribbean.

FURTHER INFORMATION

BOOKS TO READ

The Amazon Rainforest and its People by Marion Morrison (Hodder Wayland, 1993)

Antonio's Rainforest by Anna Lewington (Hodder Wayland, 1998)

Closer Look at the Rainforest by Selina Wood (Franklin Watts, 1996)

Geography Detective: Rainforest by Philip Sauvain (Zöe Books, 1996)

Journey into the Rainforest by Tim Knight (Oxford University Press, 2001)

Jungle by Theresa Greenaway (Dorling Kindersley, 1994)

People of the Rainforests by Anna Lewington and Edward Parker (Hodder Wayland, 1997)

The Rainforest by Karen Liptak (Biosphere Press, 1993)

Secrets of the Rainforest by Michael Chinery (Cherrytree, 2001)

WEBSITES

There are many websites about the rainforests. Type in key words to search for the information you need, or visit the following sites:

Passport to the Rainforest
http://www.passporttoknowledge.com/rainforest/main.html
Includes map, graphics, images and information about plants and animals.

Rainforest Action Network
http://www.ran.org/
Facts about rainforest people and animals presented in a question and answer format. Includes action that children can take to conserve the rainforests.

Rainforest Conservation Fund
http://www.conservacion.org/
Provides species data for plants and animals. There is also news, projects and articles.

Rainforest Information Centre
http://www.forests.org/ric/
News, information, ecology and conservation. Includes a links page for children.

Species Survival Network CITES Conference
http://www.defenders.org/cites.html
Information on CITES conferences, which discuss the world's endangered species. It includes appendixes of endangered animals and plants.

World Rainforest Movement
http://www.wrm.org.uy/
Includes information on rainforests by country and by subject.

WWF–UK
http://www.wwf-uk.org/
In addition to its main website in the UK, the environmental organization has a number of sites devoted to different campaigns.
http://www.panda.org/
The international site for WWF.
http://www.panda.org/forest4life
The forests for life campaign.

Visit learn.co.uk for more resources

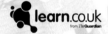

VIDEO

Baka: People of the Rainforest by Phil Agland (DJA River Films for Channel 4, 1987)

ADDRESSES OF ORGANIZATIONS

Friends of the Earth, 26-28 Underwood Street, London N1 7JQ Tel: 0207 490 1555
Web: http://www.foe.co.uk/
Greenpeace, Canonbury Villas, London N1 2PN Tel: 020 7865 8100
http://www.greenpeace.org.uk/
Oxfam, Oxfam House, Banbury Road, Oxford, OX2 7DZ Tel: 01865 312610
http://www.oxfam.org.uk/
Survival International, 6 Charterhouse Buildings, London EC1M 7ET Tel: 0207 687 8700
http://www.survival-international.org/
WWF–UK, Panda House, Weyside Park, Godalming, Surrey GU7 1XR Tel: 01483 426444
http://www.wwf-uk.org/

INDEX

Picture acknowledgements:
All photographs are by Edward Parker with the exception of the following: B & C Alexander 7; Still Pictures 4 bottom, 8 (Herbert Giradet), 19 (Mark Edwards), 24 (Nigel Dickinson). Artwork is by Peter Bull.